POWER PROSPECTING

How to gain access to key decision makers

Mark Satterfield

Mandalay Press ■ Alpharetta , GA

ISBN 0-9724715-0-2

Published by 720 Rio Grande Drive, Alpharetta, GA 30022.

Cover design © TLC Graphics and Tom Knauss

Interior design © TLC Graphics, www.TLCGraphics.com

Printed in U.S.A.

First printing, October 2002

*To my wife, Marian, for all her love,
unshakable faith and support.*

Table of Contents

Introduction

Carl faced a challenge. While his competitors consistently achieved record sales, Carl's group struggled. Carl lay awake at nights wondering what was wrong. He felt that a large part of the problem was his team's inconsistent approach to prospecting. Sure they were willing to prospect when he hovered over their shoulder and made it a strong monthly mandate. However, once sales slightly improved, prospecting activity dried up completely. How could he make prospecting an integral part of his team's day to day activities?

Cheryl's sales team faced a different challenge. They enthusiastically embraced the concept of prospecting, at least on an intellectual basis. However, when it came time to actually implement a prospecting strategy, they floundered. "We had a general sense for the components of a prospecting strategy; networking, increasing our professional visibility and the effective use of the telephone, yet, we were clueless about how to really implement the process. Nothing seemed to actually generate new business. After a while we were ready to give up."

Alex's company relied on the rainmaking capabilities of a few top performers. The business they generated trickled down and provided lots of opportunities for the field sales force to manage the on-going client relationships. This worked fine until two of the rainmakers left the company. In quick order the pipeline of new accounts dried up. Realizing that new business development would now be a priority, Alex embarked on a strategy to drive new business. Although he was aware of the various means by which to generate new business, Alex was unsure how effective each one would be. Thus, he embarked on a sequential testing strategy in which each method would be tested independently to determine if it worked. Alex's plan was to focus his team's efforts on the tactic that worked the best. "After all, why waste our time on doing everything if there's one method that's the best?" Six months later Alex felt he was no closer to finding the "magic answer" than he was when he started.

Rainmakers, top guns, power prospectors, business builders, new-logo builders, call them what you will. If there is one challenge that consumes sales executives it's, "How do I turn more of my team into this type of sales professional?" Rainmakers know how to keep the pipeline filled with new customers, which is the lifeblood of any organization. Recruiting experienced top guns from outside the company is enormously expensive and seldom works out in the long term. This raises a number of challenges. How can I create more rainmakers on my team? How can I become one? What exactly do the top rainmakers *do* that makes them so successful?

To answer these questions I studied top business developers from 11 different industries. These were all individuals nominated by their management for being particularly successful at generating new business. To gain an appreciation for what did not work, I also interviewed individuals for whom prospecting had been identified as a developmental need. This research was supplemented by insights I've gained over the past ten years working with sales teams in a variety of industries. What makes a successful rainmaker? Is the ability inherent or can it be taught? Are there special skills that make someone successful at gaining access and selling to key decision-makers, or is sales just sales? What I found was that the individuals who were the most successful in selling to key decision-makers did have a set of special skills.

Who exactly were these key decision-makers? Typically, they were either the CEO or someone who reported directly to that individual. There were some instances where the nature of what was being sold did not lend itself to selling at the most senior levels. However, even in these instances, the rainmakers still prospected at a level higher than their competitors. Top business developers were not easily intimidated. Says Jason Plum, a successful sales professional in the technology industry, "It's a lot easier to start high and work your way down, than vice versa." This book will teach you what they did, how they did it and how to apply what made them successful to your own individual situation.

Traits & Characteristics of Top Business Developers

It is very apparent that first and foremost, prospecting has to be a part of your daily routine if you sincerely want to become a rainmaker. It can't be something you do only when the pipeline of new business dries up. While maintaining enthusiasm for new business development is not always easy, for top rainmakers it's an activity that never stops.

Arthur Blackspure is a great example of this. At the age of 70 he's still one of the top rainmakers for his company. He's managed to successfully overcome an issue common with many older workers, building relationships with people considerably younger than himself. For example, most people in their 20s tend to forge relationships with others in their 20s, when they're in their 30s, their strongest bonds are with others in their 30s, and so on. Obviously if you limit your relationships to people the same age as yourself, as you approach retirement all of your contacts are also likely to be retiring. This is fine if you want to retire, but a potential career killer if you don't. Throughout his career Arthur made a concerted effort to develop relationships with younger people who were on the fast track at their companies. These relationships have enabled Arthur to be a top producer for over five decades.

What else made a difference between those who were successful at rainmaking and those that were not? Although it might sound obvious, one key differentiating factor is calling on the right person. Rainmakers have a remarkably accurate understanding about who has influence and who doesn't. We need to know who the real decision-maker is, and not be fooled by the person who says they're the decision-maker, when in fact they're not.

Not surprisingly, rainmakers have considerable knowledge about their own products and services. While that's important, it's also pretty basic. What distinguished the rainmakers was the depth of knowledge they had about their clients' industries. They understood with great clarity what the issues were that kept their clients awake at night. They also were very well versed on what their clients' competition was up to. I'll discuss in more detail how rainmakers went about collecting this information and how they used this data to build successful relationships.

It is one thing to consider yourself an expert, but quite another to be considered an expert by your prospects and customers. There's an old but true saying that you aren't an expert unless others know that you're one. How does one become an expert? Rainmakers used speaking and writing as the two primary vehicles to build their reputations. While less successful sales people understood that writing articles and giving speeches would help them be perceived as an expert, they never got around to actually doing anything. Rainmakers did more than just talk a good game. They actually wrote articles and made presentations.

What about the methods used to meet those of influence? Not surprisingly the most common method was through networking. One would think that with as much that has been written about networking, that we would be a society of wonderful networkers. Unfortunately, we're not. Very few people actually do a particularly good job of networking. There is a real methodology for successful networking that the top players understood and implemented.

Another important characteristic of our top business developers was that they never lost touch with someone who they felt could be helpful. Staying in contact requires both organization and creativity. This is particularly true if one's product or service doesn't change on a regular basis. It's not that difficult for me to determine what to say the first time I call you. But what's my excuse to call you the second time, or the time after that? How do I stay in frequent contact without becoming a pest?

The answer lies in a using a variety of creative excuses in order to stay in touch. These might include insights on a project, input on an article, recommending a top job candidate, passing along a piece of industry intelligence or offering some valuable insights on issues impacting your prospect's business. If you put your mind to it, you can come up with a lot of excuses like these to stay in touch. For example, in the process of writing this book I've been in contact with dozens of my clients and prospects to get their thoughts and ideas. Not only do these conversations give me valuable insights, but they also serve as excuses to stay in contact.

Applying the Power Prospecting Tactics to Your Own Sales Situation

Any type of sales training is only valuable if you apply what you're learning to an actual sales challenge that you're facing. I want this book to be more than just a passive learning experience. My goal is for you to apply the tactics I'll be discussing so you can move your business forward. With that thought in mind, I'd like for you take out a pad of paper. On the top of the first page write the name of an account. It can be one that you're currently working on or perhaps one that you're planning to build a relationship with. Either is fine, just so long as it's an account that's important to you. If you keep this pad of paper with you and complete the exercises as you read this book, you'll have a wealth of tactics and ideas that you can begin to immediately implement. Let's now spend some time getting to know the key people on the account that you just wrote down.

Two Groups of Influence

One of the challenges that many business developers face is getting to the key decision-maker. The issues are very common. "I don't know who the decision-maker is." "The purchasing agent said I should just deal with her." "I get intimidated by dealing with a senior level person." "I don't have credibility with people at that level." "All her calls are screened." When we look at these challenges we find that they fall into three major categories.

First, you may be having difficulty identifying the decision-maker. Secondly, you may be blocked from getting to the person who can really make the decision. Third, many people feel anxious or uncomfortable when they're actually in front of a senior level decision-maker. We'll discuss strategies to help you in all three of these areas.

Let's talk about the first area, identifying the decision-maker. Think about the people at your prospective client as falling into one of two groups. The first is the decision-maker. This may be a single individual, or if you sell a variety of products, there may be multiple decisions-makers. The decision-maker is the one who can, as the name would indicate, actually make the decision to buy your product or use your services.

The second, and much larger group, includes supervisors, users of the product and technical experts. We'll refer to this second group by the acronym **S**(supervisors), **U**(users), **TE**(technical experts) or **SUTE**s. These are people who can influence the purchasing decision but don't actually have the authority to make the decision. That doesn't mean that they're not important. However, their needs are different than those of the decision-maker and we will need to cultivate our relationships with them differently. It's important that we don't get confused about who does what. Those who claim they are the decision-maker often do so in the hopes that we won't circumvent the process by going over their heads. Others claim to be the decision-maker for ego reasons, or simply because they feel that they *might* be able to make the decision. Unless we're sure about the level of influence each individual has in the company, it's very hard to maximize our effectiveness.

The first step is to make sure that we fully understand what we mean by decision-maker. The bottom line is that the decision-maker is the individual who can make the decision without further approval. Think of it this way. When you submit your invoice, who will have to sign off on it in order for you to get paid? That person is the decision-maker. Never lose sight of that target. That's not to say that you want to just exclusively focus on influencing him or her. That would be short sighted. Decisions are not made in a vacuum and any good decision-maker is going to want input from those who are likely to be impacted by the decision to buy your product or service.

How do we identify the decision-makers? One method that we will discuss in more detail later, is to purchase contact names from a list broker. An alternative to this is to hire a recruiting researcher to develop an organization chart on a company that's a top prospect. The executive search community has used this practice for many years and there's no reasons why you can't make it work for you. You can find individuals who do this type of work through Kennedy Publications, which publishes a directory of these researchers. You can buy this directory from Kennedy at www.kennedyinfo.com.

If you're targeting specific industries you might want to consider buying one of the many directories published by Dun & Bradstreet. They do a good job of keeping their information current and the price is very reasonable. Each listing provides a variety of contacts. This is helpful if the decision-maker you're trying to contact isn't at the top of the organization, or if you sell to multiple departments in a company. More information can be found at their website, www.dnb.com.

It's also important to remember that the decision-maker is likely to change over time. Just because a person is the decision-maker today, doesn't mean that they'll play the same role the next time around. There are a number of factors that will influence this. For example, the more you're asking them to spend-the higher the decision will be made in the organization. Similarly, as business conditions become more difficult, the higher the decision is likely to be made. Another factor is your personal history with the client. If the company knows you or your firm they may feel more comfortable delegating the purchasing decision down in the organization. If you're an unknown entity, the opposite is often true.

One of our clients sells a training program to a large multinational bank. When they started working with the bank, the decision to use their service was made at an extremely high level. As the company became more comfortable with the supplier the decision making process became less arduous and was delegated to more junior level people.

This presents its own unique challenges. How does one remain in contact with the senior level individuals when they're no longer directly involved in the approval process? New reasons or excuses need to be created in order to stay in touch. Developing these high level relationships is so difficult and time consuming that one doesn't want them to lapse due to lack of contact. However, if I just call to thank the high level executive for renewing the contract she'll think that I'm wasting her time. Once you waste the time of someone at this level it's very hard to regain your credibility. Thus, success with a client creates its own set of challenges. We'll discuss creative strategies to deal with this situation shortly.

As I mentioned, there is a second group of individuals who play a variety of roles in the decision. These are the people we referred to as the SUTEs. Who are they?

The SUTEs have varying degrees of influence ranging from considerable to negligible. They don't decide who wins, but they do have a say about who can play. In effect they limit the number of participants. The SUTEs tend to focus on the product itself and evaluate it based on factors such as, ease of use, compatibility with existing systems, or will your product make them look good in the eyes of their superiors? By contrast, the decision-makers tend to evaluate products or services from a broad strategic perspective. Issues for them might include, lowering overall costs, impact on profitability or gaining market share.

Where should you focus your initial efforts? At the decision-maker or on the SUTEs? It is far better to aim too high than too low. Starting at the top and working your way down is always preferable to attempting to push the boulder up the hill. This strategy also is helpful to avoid getting blocked from dealing with the decision-maker.

It is very difficult for a SUTE to shut you out from communicating with the decision-maker if you've already had interaction with him or her. Ultimately, your strategy should be to gain the confidence of the SUTE and convince her that you are truly looking for a win-win outcome. We'll discuss the specifics on how you do this shortly.

On your pad of paper, underneath where you wrote down the name of the account, write down the name of the person who you believe is the decision-maker. If you're uncertain about who the decision-maker is, simply write down DM with a large question mark next to it. This will remind you that finding out *who* that person is should be high on your list of priorities. Next write down at least three SUTEs for this account. These should be people who can influence the decision, although that level of influence is likely to vary from person to person. Don't feel constrained to write down the names of only three SUTEs. This is a good opportunity to list as many SUTEs as you can.

Once you've listed the decision-maker and a minimum of three SUTEs, assign to each of them a level of influence.

This is simply whether you believe that the person has a high, medium or low influence on the buying decision. Obviously the person you've chosen as the decision-maker will have a high degree of influence. The level of influence for your three SUTEs may vary considerably. Naturally, this is only a snapshot of what you believe to be their levels of influence at *this* moment in time. As you learn new information about these people, or as their roles change, you'll want to adjust your contact strategy accordingly.

What Influences Your Prospect's Decision to Buy?

"One of the concerns I had about calling on key decision-makers was determining what I was going to say. My experience had been selling much lower in the organization and I considered myself pretty effective at the standard features and benefits presentation. I knew that this wasn't going to be enough if I was fortunate to get the attention of the top person.

Over time (and more than a few botched attempts) I was able to determine what was important to these senior level executives. Although it varied somewhat depending on who I was talking with, the key areas of concern included; increased efficiencies, growing market share, reducing expenses and increasing shareholder satisfaction. Once I figured this out, I was able to align the benefits of my products and services with what was top of mind with the senior executive. It was a subtle rather than dramatic shift in how I sold. I truly think it made me more effective. If nothing else, it raised my confidence level that I was communicating on the same level as the person I was talking with. This made me, at least in my own mind, equal in stature to the top person."

— *Tim Lang, Technology Consulting*

The more you know about the individuals on your account the more effective you'll be at managing the account as a whole. The more knowledgeable you are about this particular account the more you'll be able to make accurate judgements about the issues that affect other companies in the same industry. For example, if managing supply chain relationships is an issue for your client, it's possible or even likely that this may be an issue for other companies in the same industry. If nothing else, it will give you a bona fide reason for calling other companies to determine if they are facing the same issues. Having assisted one company in an industry goes a long way towards establishing your credibility with others in similar fields.

Although your long-term strategy should be to become an industry expert, it's important to remember that sales is an intensely personal process. Companies don't really buy from companies as much as people buy from other people. The client really isn't Citibank; it's Nancy who's a senior executive in the finance department. Thus, it's very important that you have a deep understanding of what motivates your decision-maker and the SUTEs. In order for the strategies and tactics we'll talk about later to work, this foundation has to be firmly in place.

Business success and personal achievement are usually intertwined. This is important to keep in mind during the sales process, since individuals usually will not agree to a business decision unless they feel that it's both in their own personal interest *and* in the best interest of their company. As an extreme example, getting a prospect to buy a product that could result in the elimination of his job is a highly difficult sale. Prospects are most likely to buy products and services if, 1) it helps their company achieve its goals, and, 2) helps them as individuals achieve a personal goal. We refer to the first as business results and the second as personal wins. We need to discover what constitutes results and wins for everyone who has influence on our account.

What might a result be for the decision-maker? It could be increased efficiency, greater market share or an increased percentage of repeat customers. Other results might include greater employee utilization, reducing the cost of sales, or lowering expenses. These are all business results that are of importance to decision-makers.

Results for the SUTEs are somewhat different. These results tend to be much more user-oriented or technically oriented results. Is your product easily adaptable to the existing system? Will it be easy to use or will it be cumbersome? In short, how much of a hassle will it be to implement the changes that will be required if I buy your products?

Successful sales professionals understand the differences between what constitutes a result for a decision-maker vs. a SUTE. The more you can tailor your communications to the specific needs of your audience, the more effective you'll be. For example, if you discuss technical specifications and ease of training with the decision-maker, she probably won't particularly care. Conversely, if you talk about how your product fits into the broad business objectives of the organization, the SUTE might find the discussion to be intellectually interesting, but it won't relate to the specific reasons for why he should buy your products. Successful communication of results depends upon tailoring what you say to meet the business interests of the person you're speaking with.

In addition to results there are also what we call Wins. Wins are personal. These might include; having more leisure time, increasing self-esteem, avoiding a relocation, obtaining more organizational power, increasing job security, being viewed as a problem solver or being perceived as a leader.

Sometimes knowing about a Win helps you directly move the business forward, and sometimes the benefit is more subtle and longer term. For example, having worked for many years in the food industry I have a strong relationship with many of the large consumer goods companies. One particular CEO was dissatisfied with his current employment situation and was shopping around quietly for new opportunities. This CEO used me as a sounding board to discuss potential career options. My thoughts and feedback certainly went a long ways towards building my credibility as a professional in his eyes. Since he appreciated my input on career issues it made him highly receptive to taking my phone calls during this important period in his life. I firmly believe that the time I invested with him during his job search was a contributing factor in the positive business relationship that exists today.

Turn again to the list you made previously of the contacts for your account. For each person of influence, write down what would constitute a result and a win for that person. If you're not clear on a result or win put a large question mark next to the name. This will serve as a reminder that this is information you need to collect.

If you are successful in developing a wealth of knowledge about results and wins for the people on your account, you're in a wonderful position to build credibility and influence. If you invest the time to identify results and wins, you'll notice that the relationship between you and your client changes. This is because you have developed a

POWER PROSPECTING | 15

client focused perspective. It's highly likely that the relationship will move from that of customer and vendor to one of two colleagues intent upon building a mutually beneficial business relationship. As you erase barriers between yourself and the SUTE, the likelihood of him blocking your access to senior management also dramatically decreases. This occurs because you are no longer viewed as a threat, but rather as a resource who can help the SUTE achieve his or her business and personal goals.

Managed correctly, this is a process in which everyone benefits. However, in order to be successful you have to understand what motivates the contacts on your account. This can't be accomplished in a casual or sporadic manner. Obtaining information about wins and results needs to be a top priority of yours every time you have interaction with those of influence.

Keeping Track of Your Prospects

All of the strategies, tactics and communication skills are for naught if you don't have a system in place to track your prospecting activity. There are a host of options available, ranging from customer relationship management systems (CRM), to sales force automation systems to fundamental contact management software. What's best for you will depend on how large your sales team is and the size of the companies you sell to. If you're engaged in a true enterprise sales effort, in which you're selling cross-functional capabilities to a very large client, a CRM system may be the way to go. However, for most of us, CRM is analogous to using a nuclear bomb to kill a nest of fire ants. It just isn't designed for most selling situations. The key with any prospecting tracking system is that you need to actually use it. If it's not simple and easy, you won't.

I'm often asked what system do I use? Since I don't need to extensively coordinate prospecting activities across multiple professionals, the contact management system ACT works just fine. I like it because it's easy to input data, enables me to keep track of past activities and reminds me of future initiatives that I don't want to forget. Plus, I can use it with my Palm Pilot to update activities when I'm on the road. You can find out more about ACT by visiting their website at www.act.com.

My advice is to start small and trade up as your needs expand. Too large a system too early will crash under its own weight. On the opposite extreme you don't want to try to keep all of your follow-up activities in your head. That's impossible. If you're serious about becoming a rainmaker, you'll very quickly expand your activities beyond what can realistically be managed in your head or on a pad of paper.

Now, let's take a look at more issues that impact our prospect's decision to buy.

Understanding Your Prospect's Readiness To Buy

A nother consideration is understanding the client's readiness to buy. While we may not have a great amount of control over this, it's important that we understand the client's buying mindset. It can take four different forms.

The first is what's called the Building Mindset. The client views their current situation as one in which there is opportunity for growth. When a client is in a building mindset they are ready to buy goods or services that can help them achieve the results they want. However, just because they are in a mode where they are receptive to buying, this is no guarantee that they will buy from you. Knowing that the client is in a building mindset enables you to position your products to their greatest advantage.

Conversely, there are times when your client is in Pain. Again, the client is in the mode of needing to buy goods and services, but they will buy from the person who can eliminate the pain the *quickest*. Speedy removal of the pain is the primary objective of the client. Given a choice between building and pain, you can rest assured that alleviating pain will always take precedent over building. Not being aware of whether your prospect is in a building or pain mindset is often a common problem. Although you may assume that the client is in one mindset you need to be prepared to quickly shift gears if it becomes apparent that your initial assumption is incorrect.

There's an old story about the salesperson that tries to sell a new roof to a farmer whose barn is on fire. It's not that the farmer isn't going to need a new roof, he just doesn't need one now!

The advantage of having clients in either a pain or building mindset is that you know they're going to be open to buying services that will help them grow their businesses or alleviate the pain. The most challenging buying mode is what we call Happy State. That's when the needs of the customer are pretty well served by the products or services he's currently using. When the client is in this happy state there are a couple of things we can try to reinvigorate the need to buy.

The first is to let them know about trouble or pain that may be headed their way. In order to be credible, the more you can discuss specific examples of the problems others are facing in their industry, the more attention you're going to get. Naturally, in order for this strategy to be effective you've got to be completely up to speed on what's going on in their industry. You've got to be reading what your customers are reading, attending the professional association meetings, and learning about the issues that are of most importance to them. We'll talk about all of these in more detail a little later.

While giving your clients insights about the future is one strategy to move them off the happy mindset, an alternative strategy is to readjust their thinking about their business performance. This is particularly effective when you know that your client's competitors are achieving greater levels of success than your client is.

"Yes Ms. Client what you're achieving is good, however I must tell you that Your Chief Competitor just reported earnings that are 15% greater. We've done some investigating about how they achieved those results and I think we could help you do the same or better."

Either of these strategies gives you a fighting chance of getting your client out of the happy state and into a position where they are interested in learning more about your products or services. Think about it from your own company's perspective. Even if you were satisfied and content, if I came to you with information about why your competitors are more successful, wouldn't you want to know how they're getting those results?

When a client is in the happy mindset it's generally easier to sell growth than it is pain avoidance. Unfortunately, we are usually short sighted and hope that bad events won't hit us directly. It's far more fun and sexy to grow a business than it is to focus on problems. It's one of those terrible ironies that it's very difficult to sell pain unless the person is actually experiencing it. However, if you have an appreciation for both mindsets you can quickly switch gears and position your presentation in a way that is most likely to be received favorably.

The fourth mindset is Fantasy Land, and unfortunately there isn't too much you can do when your client is in this mindset, except wait. In the fantasy land mode the client thinks they are doing wonderfully, when in fact their results are terrible. Reality just hasn't hit them yet. They're living in a dream world. Although there is nothing you can do short-term to change their mind, the good news is that sooner or later reality *will* hit and then the prospect will be in the pain mode they so richly deserve.

From a strategic standpoint you want to know the buying mode of your clients since this will give you clues for your speeches and articles. One of the challenges people face when they prepare a presentation or begin to write an article is that they don't know what to speak or write about. A helpful idea is to focus on the business issues your clients are facing and the kinds of results they're looking for. In other words, discuss the buying mode that they're in. If you follow this strategy it is likely that your article or speech will have a broad industry appeal, since if something pains one company, there's a high probability that others are also impacted.

Now is a good time to write down some notes on what you feel to be the buying mindset of the people on your account. Remember that the mindset can vary from person to person. We often read about a particular industry or company that is experiencing significant growth or contraction. Does that mean that everyone at that company is furiously buying everything they can get their hands on, or conversely, that all purchasing has come to a complete halt? Of course not. Although the overall account may have a particular mindset, what is really important is the mindset of the individual. Remember that companies don't buy products or services, people do. It's not General Motors that's buying your services, it's Betty in the IT department or Hal in the accounting area. Sales are personal.

As a result you want to take with the proverbial grain of salt what the business press says about the industry you sell to. For example, we do a lot of work in the telecommunications industry. As I write this chapter everything I read about the telecom business is that it's doing poorly. If I followed blindly what I read, I wouldn't waste my time trying to sell to the telecom industry and would instead focus my energies on industries like biotech and oil & gas. Interestingly, I market to all three of these industries and this year telecom will be my largest client. That's strictly due to the relationships I've developed and the ability to position my services in a way that resonates with the buying needs of these clients. Now that's not to say that one should ignore what's reported in the business press, but you should put it in perspective. Draw your conclusions from multiple data points. The bottom line is that you should make sure that you have a firm understanding of the buying mindset of the individuals on your account, the account as a whole *and* the industry your account is in.

The Importance of Focus and Specialization

Mary Haven, who is a top rainmaker for her manufac-turing firm believes that she gets her calls returned because her clients know that she has a wealth of knowledge about what's going on in her industry. She can discuss business trends as well as who's been promoted, demoted or changed jobs. This type of industry knowledge, or gossip, is very enticing. Taking a telephone call from Mary is really an opportunity to get updated on trends and who's doing what in her industry.

Mary supplements her reputation by writing frequently for an industry trade publication and speaking at conferences, meetings and symposiums. She uses her speeches as a tool for staying in touch by calling existing and prospective clients and encouraging them to attend. Writing articles both enhances Mary's credibility and provides her with a variety of excuses for staying in touch with her clients, both when she is researching the article and after it is published.

Focus is an important component in developing your reputation for expertise. Most people define their focus by industry. Others define it by function or by what department typically buys their services. Finally, others may have a geographical focus. Naturally, focus can be some combination of these three. It's important to have a focus, otherwise it's very hard to become an expert. If you don't, it's a little like saying let's go eat American food. It just doesn't limit your choices significantly in order to target your efforts.

Joining What Your Prospects Join

Once you've determined where to focus the next step is to join the group that caters to that industry or function. If you're unclear on what association serves these groups, the answer is as near as your computer. Go on-line and access the search engine Google (www.google.com). Type in the industry or function you want, followed by the word, association. In a matter of moments you'll see a vast list of potential groups that cater to your search criteria. It will probably take you a little bit of time to investigate the various sites that are listed, and it's likely you will run down a few blind alleys. However, with a modicum of effort you should be able come up with multiple associations that are worth investigating. Another benefit of this search process is that you will uncover special, one-time events that you might want to attend. For example, during a recent Google search I came across a conference for senior level sales leaders, sponsored by one of the Ivy League universities. This is an exceptional opportunity for me to network with a group of top decision-makers who would be very difficult for me to contact through more traditional methods. I'd encourage you to put down this book and get on-line with Google right now and see what your research turns up!

Reading What Your Prospects Read

The second strategy of successful rainmakers was that they read what their targeted group of prospects read. Naturally, in order to do this they first had to find out what their prospects were reading. Fortunately, this is pretty simple and straightforward. The easiest way to find out is to simply ask your clients what they read. This is a good excuse or reason to stay in touch with your clients and it sends a very positive message about your personal commitment to their industry. Also pay attention to what magazines are lying around in the reception area the next time you call on your client. This not only gives you information about what your clients read but who else sells to this group of prospects.

When you're reading these magazines or trade journals you'll want to make sure that you're reading them from a marketer's perspective. How can what I'm reading help me build my business? An interesting point of fact is that few people who are mentioned in the press are ever contacted by individuals seeking their business.

This point was driven home a few days ago. I was in a local bookstore and happened to browse the magazine rack. I picked up a copy of the Harvard Business Review and noticed that there was an article in it by an old colleague of mine. Of course I was thoroughly impressed to know someone who was published in such a prestigious magazine, and took it upon myself to give this person a call a few days later. I knew that the magazine had been on the racks for the better part of a month, so I was interested in how many other people had called the author to congratulate him or to seek his business. I wasn't terribly surprised when in response to my question the author replied, "How many people have contacted me? You mean aside from my mother? Just you." The point is that hardly anyone contacts people who appear in print, and that's a shame. It's easy to write the author of an article you're impressed with a short note, and if you don't know the address, you can send it to them in care of the publication. It's an easy and highly productive method to establish contact with people who would be difficult to get in touch with by other means.

Along these same lines it's helpful to establish relationships with the business reporters who cover your industry. For example, since a lot of my work is with technology companies and consulting firms, I've made it a point to get to know the reporters who cover these areas. By being a source to them I've been able to establish relationships that are mutually beneficial. They get quotes and insights into the goings-on in these industries, and I get tips about personnel changes, mergers and relocations. I'm a little surprised that none of my competitors have tried to strike up similar relationships with these reporters.

Something else you'll want to pay attention to as you're perusing the trade publications is who is advertising? Again this is an often-overlooked area of opportunity.

I do a fair amount of business with one of the largest technology consulting firms in the country largely because they happened to run an advertisement in a trade journal. This particular ad listed the name of the regional VP and gave his phone number. That prompted me to give this person a call in which I referenced the ad and how effective I thought it was. This initial call ultimately resulted in an introduction to their national head of training. Today, this consulting firm is a valued client of my firm.

As I'm preparing this I'm looking at a recent copy of the *Atlanta Business Chronicle*. These Business Chronicles, which appear in a large number of U.S. cities, do a wonderful job of reporting on local business activities. The issue I'm looking at has an interesting ad in it for the luxury marketing council. The ad lists its members, which are a prestigious group including the Ritz Carlton, Rolex and other high profile organizations. If I were selling to the luxury market this would be an organization I would definitely consider joining. You can pick up some interesting marketing ideas simply by paying attention to who is advertising.

I used to think that if I actually contacted people who were quoted in the press or wrote articles they would think I was a pest. I incorrectly assumed that they got bombarded with telephone calls. Ironically, the exact opposite is true. Moreover, when you introduce yourself and say that you really enjoyed their article, it's a very positive way to begin a business relationship.

Monitoring the Comings and Goings in Your Industry

P romotions and personnel announcements. Are you tracking these by reading the appropriate business publications? If not, you really should be.

One way of keeping up to date on the comings and goings of people in your industry is by monitoring the websites run by the professional associations. They do a good job of tracking who just got promoted or changed companies. On my to-do list every morning is to check key association websites to see who has moved. This personnel intelligence gives me a creative reason to introduce myself.

I also make sure I log onto Hunt Scanlon's website at www.huntscanlon.com to check out promotions and personnel announcements on a national scale. For example, this week I noticed that a new person just got promoted to VP of sales at a company on my hit list of prospective clients. This is the type of intelligence I need in order to ensure that I'm continuing to build my business by making new contacts every day. Hunt Scanlon's web site not only offers daily updates on executive personnel changes but also provides links to the companies mentioned in the announcements. This makes it very easy to go directly to the site and conduct some immediate intelligence gathering.

When I come across an announcement that I want to follow up on, I cut it out or print the announcement and run it through my plastic laminating machine. I like to use the plastic laminating machine since it adds a touch of class to my mailing and makes it memorable without it appearing goofy. I send the announcement with the following letter:

Dear _____ ,

I read recently about your new assignment and wanted to offer my congratulations. I wish you much success for the future and thought that you might enjoy a copy of the announcement.

By way of introduction, I'm a partner with the consulting firm Solution Resources. Our expertise is helping sales organizations make the process of prospecting for new clients more productive and less frustrating. Some of our clients include…(names the recipient would respect)

I know from talking with other heads of sales, that many of them are frustrated that new business development activities aren't conducted in a consistent and ongoing manner. We've been successful in showing our clients how to institutionalize prospecting behavior into their corporate cultures and provide them with a game plan to implement the business development strategy. If this is an issue you're wrestling with, I'd like to arrange a brief meeting to share with you how others in our industry are addressing this issue and see if we might be of assistance to you.

Again, congratulations on your new assignment. I look forward to talking with you soon.

Regards,

Mark Satterfield

Naturally, you'll want to modify this letter to meet your own personal needs but feel free to use this one as a template.

I've discovered over the years that of all the letters I send out, this one results in the highest percentage of people who are willing to take my calls when I follow up. This has consistently been one of my most effective methods to establish new relationships.

I've also gotten in the habit of asking these prospects how many other calls they received when the announcement came out? Guess what I hear? Again, hardly anyone calls these people to congratulate them and that's a shame, especially since it's such a positive way in which to start a relationship.

Websites: A Powerful Tool for Intelligence Gathering

I've mentioned before a great resource for tracking personnel changes, especially if your business is national in scope, is Hunt Scanlon's website. They also sell a directory of contacts that enables you to access names of CEOs, CIOs, HR executives or heads of sales. We subscribe to it, and it's quite good. If you're selling on a national basis it's worth investigating.

Speaking of websites, I hope you've spent some quality time visiting your client's site. I'm always surprised when people admit to me that they haven't done so. I view websites as an extension of the printed materials that cover my client's industry. You'll want to get in the habit of not only visiting the websites of your clients but also the sites for your client's competition. These habits will really help keep you abreast of issues impacting that industry. A wonderful part about most company websites is that they have a category usually titled, "us in the news" or "news for investors". These sections are great because they eliminate the hassles of doing an archival search for the recent business news about your client. The companies provide this section as a service to investors. As smart rainmakers we look at these sections from an account intelligence perspective. It enables us to find out what specifically is impacting our client.

Of course, intelligence gathering is very difficult if you don't have focus. The more focused you are, the more effective you're going to be. This is what's referred to as the deep and narrow strategy. If I try to sell my services to everyone, it's hard to develop a deep and narrow strategy. Conversely, it's relatively easy for me to keep on top of the IT community in the southeast, or the financial industry in the northeast. That's doable.

Now is a good time to start your to-do list of specific actions you'll want to take to build your rainmaking capabilities. At the top of a new sheet of paper write down what you believe your clients are reading. If you don't know, or aren't sure, write down "WHAT ARE MY PROSPECTS READING?" in capital letters and great big question mark. This will remind you that this is something you want to find out as soon as possible. Other items for your to-do list might include:

- Conduct a Google search for associations that focus on the industry you sell to.
- Visit your client's website.
- Visit the websites of your client's competitors.
- Visit the websites of your own competition.

We often overlook this last to-do. You can get lots of good information from your competitor's websites. Sometimes I pick up new and interesting ideas that I think might be interesting to try, and I'm sure that they do the same with mine.

Gaining Professional Visibility By Getting Published

A s the old saying goes, you're not an expert unless somebody else says that you are. The professionals I interviewed who were the most successful at prospecting were highly visible. How did they achieve this status? It probably won't come as any great surprise that they did it by being published and by speaking.

"The first step in my campaign to build my reputation through writing was to determine what my clients read. I developed a targeted list of publications by noting the names of industry magazines that were in the reception areas and by researching the newsletters of the trade associations my clients were members of. In some cases I simply asked my clients what they read to stay current. The importance of reading what they're reading can't be understated. Not only were the publications valuable in terms of keeping up but they also gave me a sense for how to slant my submissions to maximize the likelihood that they would get published."

— *Alice Copeland, Management Consulting*

When I interviewed individuals who were not particularly successful in prospecting, one of the questions I asked them was, did they try to get published? No, they didn't write. Why not?

"I don't think I can write."

"I don't know what to write about."

"I don't have time to write."

Conversely, among the group that was successful at prospecting the vast majority had been published. Where they had been published ranged from industry newsletters to the Harvard Business Review. (Interestingly, the articles that were published in industry specific newsletters tended to generate the most business.) One of the keys to getting published was that when the rainmakers came up with an idea that they thought might make a good article, they wrote it down. Good ideas tend to pop up out of the blue. Whenever they appear, you want to make sure that you jot the idea down.

One of the nice aspects of writing an article is that many of them have extremely long shelf lives. Eight years ago I wrote an article, *Selling to the Top: Traits and Characteristics of Top Rainmakers*. You may have seen this article before. At last count it has been published in 17 publications. These include trade association publications, newsletters, web sites, electronic bulletin boards and other media outlets. It's also been directly responsible for five new clients. The ability to get your article published time and time again makes publishing a valuable investment of your time.

Where do you find places that might want to publish your article? At the top of your list would be the trade publications that specialize in your industry. To find these you'll want to peruse the Standard Rate and Data directory. You can find it on the web at www.srds.com or call them at 800-851-SRDS. The directory is a listing of all the magazines and newsletters published in the US. It's primarily used by advertising agencies to determine where to place advertising. I use it to identify places to place my articles.

Virtually every conceivable industry or function has a trade publication that caters to their specialized interests. The SRDS gives you specific information about what those people read. It's invaluable and unfortunately it's real expensive. You can save yourself some money by visiting the business reference section at a major branch of your local public library. In less than an hour you can develop a comprehensive list of magazines to target. Other resources for finding places to get your article published can be found through the Writers Digest series of directories. You can find out more about them at www.writersdigest.com

The next step is to write the editor of the publication to determine if he or she would be interested in publishing your article. The editor's name is usually listed along with other publishing information near the front or back of the particular publication. This is a letter I use:

Dear _____ ,

Enclosed is a copy of my article "Power Prospecting: How to Achieve Extraordinary Sales Success through Unconventional Tactics and Strategies". I thought it would be of interest to your readers.

I am happy to give you permission to publish this piece to which I hold all rights if you will run the brief author information box which appears at the conclusion of the article.

If space limitations preclude publishing the entire article, I hereby grant permission for you to edit it so long as the sense of the piece is maintained. If you find the current form of this article somehow inappropriate for your publication but are interested in the subject, I would be happy to write something exclusively for you. Please let me know.

If you do use this article, I would appreciate receiving a copy of the issue in which it appears.

Thank you for your consideration.

In the box I refer to in the letter, I usually include the following: Mark Satterfield is a partner with the sales training and consulting firm Solution Resources in Atlanta Georgia. The firm specializes in assisting sales teams make prospecting for new business less frustrating and more productive. He can be reached at Mark@consulting-experts.com

Once your article is published you'll want to get reprints and send them to clients, prospects and anyone else you can think of. I'm very aggressive in this regard, as are most of my colleagues. It's another way to stay out in front of the client and a powerful method to build your reputation for expertise. Additionally, when you send an article to someone, the probability of its being passed along to others in the organization is quite high.

There are a number of formulas you can use to ease the pain of beginning to write. While I've personally written over 250 articles and five books, writing is not a particularly natural activity for me. However, because I so strongly believe that being published helps me grow my business, I force myself to write on a regular basis. You'll discover that the process isn't really all that difficult once you get in the habit. Formulas can help you get started.

We've all experienced that sinking feeling you get when you look at an empty computer screen or a blank sheet of paper. Starting to write is the most difficult part of the process, and this is where formulas can help get you over that initial speed bump. There are four formulas that are worth knowing about.

The first and easiest one is the interview. You can interview colleagues, clients, prospects or even yourself, if you're so inclined. Here's a clever idea you might want to consider.

Todd Black who's in charge of business development for a large software firm in Silicon Valley, proposed writing a regular column entitled "The Winner's Profile". It consisted of a short 300-word profile of leading executives in his industry. The benefits to Todd are numerous. It enables him to contact high profile prospects under a non-sales guise, which increases the likelihood of his call being returned. Who wouldn't want to receive free publicity and ego fulfillment by being profiled in an article like this? It was a great way to initiate a conversation, which ultimately turned into many productive business relationships. If your trade publication isn't publishing such a "winner's profile", suggest it. Smaller publications are often starving for articles and your suggestion is likely to be received extremely positively.

If you don't have a prior endorsement from the trade publication, don't let that stop you. You can write the article on "spec". That is you write the article first, and then seek places to get it published. This is how I typically work. You can pitch it this way when you call a high profile person in your industry that you want to interview.

> "Hi. This Mark Satterfield and I'm in the process of preparing an article for submission to Our Industry Trade Journal on emerging trends and was hoping I could get 20 minutes of your time to interview you for the article."

I ask for 20 minutes because it's less demanding than asking for a half-hour, but since hardly anyone actually schedules his or her time in 20-minute increments, you wind up getting at least a half-hour with the person.

Of course there is etiquette involved in this process. For example, you don't want to conduct the interview and then never actually write the article. That will come back to haunt you. On the couple of occasions where I've written an article but haven't found a place to publish it, I send a draft copy to the person I interviewed asking for their comments. Not only does this satisfy the individual's curiosity about what you wrote, but it's also another great excuse or reason to get back in contact with the person. When the article does get published, I send everyone I interviewed a copy. This is a good idea to do even if you're sure that they received a copy of the publication through other sources. It's a nice professional touch, shows your consideration, and again it's a great excuse to stay in contact!

The interview format is the easiest to write because you're writing in the same style as you speak. This is an important point, which is to write as you speak. I know the English teachers out there are going to rise up in revolt when I say not to excessively worry about grammar. Most people communicate just fine when they're speaking. This conversational style also works very well when communicating on paper. A test that one of my editors told me early in my writing career, is to read out loud what you've written. If it sounds like you speaking, it's probably fine. If it's absolutely necessary, the publication will hire an editor to clean up the language. Remember that the key to getting published is to write.

Another formula is the survey. This often takes the form of, "more and more (or less and less) people are worried about (something)". More and more. Less and less. I like the survey format because the research you do in preparation for the article puts you in direct contact with the people you want to do business with.

For example, we do a periodic survey of sales managers on the prospecting habits of successful business developers. This book and numerous articles have resulted from the research. Not only do I get a lot of valuable content, but the people I'm inviting to participate in the survey are the same people I will invite to purchase my books, tapes or attend my seminars. There's not a great deal of benefit in surveying a group of people who will never become customers.

Another format is the Alternative viewpoint. This is very effective if you would like to get a letter to the editor published. This is surprisingly easy and you don't have to be a brand named celebrity in order to get your letter published. What is important, is that you have an alternative point of view. Anytime you read an article in a trade or business publication that relates to the service or product you sell, realize that this represents an opportunity to get published. All you have to do is write a letter to the editor that advocates a different or alternative opinion. Once your letter gets published there is no reason not to get them reproduced, plastic laminated and sent off to your contact list. Again, you want to maximize the benefits from everything you do. No prospecting initiative should be a stand-alone. Everything you do should feed into something else that can help you build your business.

Yet another formula is the Case Study. This format builds on what you're probably doing currently when you're in front of a client. As you're most likely aware, anecdotal selling is one of the most powerful tools in face-to-face selling. Anecdotal selling is basically telling stories about other people who faced situations similar to your prospect, and by purchasing your products solved a problem or achieved a goal. Another nice aspect of case studies is that you can use the anecdotes and stories again and again in face-to-face selling, in your speeches and in other articles. You always want to recycle as much of what you create as possible. Everything you develop should be able to be used someplace else in the sales prospecting process. Anecdotes and stories are very powerful because of one of the basic tenants of adult education. Adults do not remember facts and figures; adults remember stories and examples

An offshoot of case studies is using lots of quotes in your articles. An advantage of using quotes is that they reduce the amount of actual creative writing that you have to do. My previously mentioned article Selling to the Top, (if you would like a free copy email me at mark@consultingexperts.com), was mostly quotes from other people. There wasn't a lot that I actually wrote from scratch. As a result it's one of the easiest formats to use since the amount of actual writing you have to do is quite small.

Formulas help speed up the process. This is important since articles can't help you build your business until they get published somewhere. Strive for production not excellence. Remember Steven Jobs' admonition to the software developers at Apple, "Real Artists Ship". It is one thing to create really cool software, but it's more important to get it in the hands of the buying public.

So, let's go back to that pad of paper with your ever-expanding list of good ideas. Turn to a fresh sheet of paper and write the word, ARTICLE at the top of the page.

A way of developing ideas for an article is to think about your prospect's mindset. What mode are they in? Are they trying to build their business and see opportunity on the horizon? Are they in pain? Perhaps their mindset is that they're in a happy state and it's your job to forecast events that can impact what they should be doing now to prepare for the future. The mindset of the prospect or client can often provide clues about the topic for an article.

Think about a goal that they're trying to reach. If one client is trying to achieve a certain goal it's likely that others are also trying to accomplish the same objective.

What's that crucial win for the client? Use these questions to jump-start your thinking and make sure you jot down ideas that come to you on your pad of paper.

Remember that there are a variety of places to submit your article for publication. These include the business press, trade journals, association newsletters, and letters to the editor. If you don't actually want to sit down and write, don't let that reluctance stop you in your quest to get published. You don't actually have to do the writing, you can hire someone to do it for you. It's done all the time. There are many services who will write what you want for a fee.

A PR firm will not only work on the writing but will also provide assistance on the placement of the article. This is usually done in the context of an overall public relations campaign. Although this is extremely professional, it winds up being a bit more than most of us realistically need or can afford. Many sales training companies, my own firm included, provide article writing services as a part of the overall direct marketing copy writing services we offer. If you want to discuss this service email me at info@consultingexperts.com

The most inexpensive method is to call the English department at your local college and ask for a student who can compose an article based on your notes, ideas or outline. You'll have to provide the student with a fairly detailed outline about the points you want to make. Using a student in this manner works particularly well if you have a lot of quotes and are looking for someone that can put them in the proper order, organize them and compose connecting sentences. If you are thinking about using the interview or survey model, hiring a student to help you edit it may be helpful.

With both writing and speaking your goal is to be perceived as an expert by your clients and prospects. However, we want to do more than just become a recognized expert. We want tangible business to come to us as a direct result of our hard work.

One way you can ensure this is when you submit your article for publication, make sure that your name and your company's name appears in the box at the conclusion of the article. You can increase the number of responses you'll get if you include your email address. People are often reluctant to call under the erroneous assumption that you're overwhelmed with adoring fans, but they will email you if you provide them with the address. I've found that most editors don't object when I ask to have it included.

Another method is to provide an incentive by offering to send them an additional report or white paper if they contact you. Once you've got them in your database you can begin the process of converting them into long term customers through the creative use of follow up letters or emails.

Money Talks: Building Your Reputation for Expertise by Speaking

"I started off speaking because I had always heard that it was a good way to build your reputation. In the beginning I would speak to anyone who would invite me. In a way that was good, because it gave me the chance to hone my speaking skills, which weren't that great in the beginning. Toastmasters and a personal coach help me gain the confidence I needed. After a while I started to develop a reputation as someone who could deliver an interesting talk and the offers started to multiply. This was somewhat of a mixed blessing. While I enjoyed the audience attention, I began to realize that there were precious few people in the audience who could potentially become clients. For a while I used the logic that everyone knew someone who might someday be a client. That was stretching the likelihood of getting business pretty far. Eventually I realized that I really was not using my time productively. I started to focus on trade associations that served my targeted group of clients. These groups were a much more productive use of my time. Speaking to these audiences both enhanced my reputation as an expert in my field and also led directly to some new accounts."

— Michael Schonefield, Electronics Distribution

Let's now shift our focus to the other part of the equation for building your reputation for expertise, public speaking. Although many people are uncomfortable with the idea of speaking before a group, it's a skill that you absolutely have to master. It's important not only for building your success in rainmaking, but also for gaining visibility with the senior management in your company. One of the most effective ways to build your organizational visibility is through making presentations, so you've got to learn the basics.

Where can you go to learn? Lots of places. Your company may have an internal presentation skills program that they offer. If they do make sure you sign up to take the class. There are also a lot of outside resources available. Perhaps the best known is Toastmasters, and it is excellent. You learn how to structure a speech and present it before an extremely supportive group of audience members. Aside from toastmasters, there are a number of training companies, mine included, that offer this type of training. Check out our website at www.consultingexperts.com to learn more about our Knock 'Em Dead Presentations program.

When you're starting your speaking career, it doesn't make a great amount of difference who's in the audience. The general rule is to speak to any group that will have you. In the beginning you just want to get experience. Public speaking is like many other things in life, it's frightening the first few time you do it, but after a little bit of experience you wonder what the big concern was.

As you develop your reputation for being able to give an interesting speech, you'll find that it's pretty easy to get speaking opportunities. At this stage in your speaking career you'll want to be selective about where you spend your time. I recently spoke to a local civic group and think I lowered the average age in the room down to about 70. It's not that they weren't a wonderful group of people, but they were all retired. Unfortunately, I can't sell sales training to the retirement set, although a few of them did promise to pass my information along to their grandkids. Maybe I'm being short sighted, but I still don't think it was the best use of my time.

Although there are no hard and fast rules to this, after you've gotten comfortable with your speaking skills, you'll want to make sure that you ask whoever is requesting your speaking services the following questions.

■ How many people will be there?

■ What's their background?

■ What's their motivation for attending?

I find that the answers to these questions are extremely helpful in determining how beneficial the speaking assignment is likely to be.

How do you get speaking assignments? The process is similar to finding places to publish your articles. First, you'll want to research where you would like to speak. We'll discuss the different types of groups you might consider when we discuss networking strategies. Once you've identified the group, you'll want to compose a letter that discusses what your topic is and why it's of important to the audience. Explain how it can help them avoid or solve a problem, and the specific benefits the audience will receive by attending. Send this to the meeting planner of the group along with your credentials. Here's a letter that I use:

Dear _____ ,

I'm a partner with the sales training and consulting firm Solution Resources. We advise sales teams on how to make their new business prospecting efforts more productive and less frustrating. Some of our clients include, (names of companies that would be of interest to their members).

We recently completed a study of the traits and characteristics of rainmakers from 11 different industries. What these successful performers had in common is the focus of my presentation. I thought that your membership might be interested in this topic and I would welcome the opportunity to address your group. My bio is attached. Please let me know if this is of interest to you.

Sincerely,

"It is very competitive to get speaking engagements, especially the good ones to the trade associations. After all, speaking to build your reputation isn't exactly a new concept. However, you don't have to be a celebrity or already be perceived as an expert in order to get engagements. It's actually a fairly straightforward process. First, I identified the groups I wanted to speak to. There are multiple directories of associations in any public library that list the dates and locations of their national and regional meetings. The associations generally work a year in advance for the national meetings and about 6 months for the large regional meetings. I would write the association's meeting chairperson about my subject. I'd stress why the topic was important and what the benefits would be to their membership. This usually took the form of how I could solve a problem they were facing or avoid a problem that might occur. With the letter I'd include my business credentials and my speaking credentials. The latter included where I had spoke previously and some testimonial letters. After I got proficient at giving speeches I had a couple of them videotaped which I then had edited into a 10-minute demo-tape. I wouldn't include the demo in the initial mailing but would send it if requested. They were requested quite often so I'm glad I made the investment. After that it was simply a matter of keeping track of where I had sent the information and following up as appropriate. "

– *Alan Barnett, Healthcare Industry*

How can you maximize the business potential of giving a speech? Rainmakers don't simply rely on someone in the audience happening to call them. By the same token we don't want to waste a lot of time with people who are unlikely to ever purchase our services and just happen to be at the meeting for the camaraderie.

What we want to do is to offer them incentives to self-nominate themselves for future contact while screening out those unlikely to actually buy our services. If you just want to collect a lot of cards you can say, "If you're interested in learning more about what I've been speaking about and would like to receive our white paper on this topic, drop off your business card in the box by the door on your way out." You'll get a lot of volume this way but will spend a lot of unproductive time calling the tire-kickers who will drop their card in any fishbowl they see.

That's why I opt for an approach that focuses more on quality rather than quantity. My approach is to ask audience members to fill out a brief survey in return for receiving the white paper or other offer. Depending on the audience I've even offered to send individuals an audio-cassette of the program if they will fill out the survey. In order to do this I simply tape record the program, duplicate it and later market the tape as a "live" presentation.

You can also use the ubiquitous evaluation form as a powerful data-gathering tool. This is an often-overlooked opportunity. For example on my evaluation form, I try to get a variety of data. First are the more commonly asked questions about what did you think about the program, what was most beneficial and what do you wish there had been more time for? Good information to get, but the answers don't directly help me build my business. Thus, I also ask if you would be interested in any of my other services such as one on one coaching, sales assessments, Knock 'Em Dead Presentation training, or my Telephone Prospecting program. I also ask if you would be interested in having this program conducted in-house at your company. Finally, I ask for names of other people I should contact regarding my services. Here's what my feedback form looks like:

Feedback Sheet

Please help us to constantly increase the VALUE of our material to you. We appreciate your filling out this form and handing it in at the end of the program.

Your name:_____

Company:_____

Address: _____

City:_____State:____Zip: _____

Phone/Email:_____

What is the BEST, most usable IDEA you gained from this program?_____

_____

_____

_____

_____

What do you wish there had been more time for? _____

_____

_____

_____

_____

Opinion of today's program: _____

_____

_____

_____

_____

May we quote you? ❑ Yes! ❑ No

Would you be interested in having this program
conducted in-house at your company? _____

Contact: _____

What else would you be interested in?

❑ Sales Assessments
❑ Knock 'Em Dead Presentations
❑ Trade Show Selling
❑ Consultative Selling
❑ Cold Calling with Confidence

Do you have a friend or business associate who would
benefit from this program?

Name: _____

Company:_____

Address: _____

City:_____State:_____Zip: _____

Phone:_____Email_____

Let me make one point about follow up. If you don't call people who fill out the survey form within two weeks, the entire effort is for naught. You will not get any business unless you follow up with prospects. It's as simple as that. No more than two weeks and ideally within one week.

Although this book is not about presentation skills, I would like to give you some brief thoughts on what makes a good presentation. One of the cardinal rules of an effective presentation is that it's chock full of stories and anecdotes. This is what makes your presentation come alive. It also helps you avoid the major problem most people have with presentations.

When you give a speech the real danger is not that you will embarrass yourself. If you practice and rehearse that hardly ever happens. The more likely problem is that no one remembers your speech 15 minutes after you give it. That's the kiss of death if you're trying to drive business through your presentations. The way to avoid this trap is to make sure that your presentation is laced with lots of stories and anecdotes. Remember my earlier comment, adults do not remember facts and figures. Adults remember examples. The big danger is that you'll bore people. Thus, always ask yourself when developing your presentation, why should the audience care? If you can't figure that out, odds are that the audience can't figure it out either. Make sure you put the interests of the audience before your desire to communicate information you know in the hope that it's of interest.

When you are developing your presentation remember the time tested structure: Tell Them What You're Going to Tell Them, Tell Them, and, Tell Them What You Told Them. It may sound trite, but successful presentations follow this structure.

For example, when I give a presentation, I start out with a summary of the traits and characteristics that make rainmakers successful. I then spend the bulk of the time in the "Tell Them" part of the presentation, in which I'm talking about those strategies in more detail. Not surprisingly at the end of the program, I'll recap and summarize the key points I've covered. This is the basic presentation structure. By following this approach you'll discover it's easy for you to organize your speech and you'll feel a lot more confident when it comes time to deliver it.

Conducting Self-Sponsored Programs to Generate New Business

You might also want to consider conducting a self-sponsored program. These are programs in which you are sponsoring the event. Executive briefings are the most common and the easiest to organize. In this format you invite people to hear about a trend, results of a survey or a study you recently conducted. This is very commonly and successfully used by consulting firms, law firms and other professional services firms. Rainmakers in other industries are also successfully using this approach as well. Another highly effective method of attracting audiences is to have a well-known guru provide the keynote address. These gurus are most easily recruited from the universities in your area. You'll have to pay the professor to speak but it's a worthwhile expense if you want to attract more senior level prospects.

"We've held a number of self-sponsored programs which have ranged from a complete bust to incredibly successful. We finally arrived on a formula that works pretty well. The programs are generally held in the afternoon. We discovered that while you can successfully run programs in the central city over breakfast or lunch, the late afternoon was best for suburban meetings since it enables participants to beat the rush-hour traffic. We would rent a meeting room at a local hotel since they are set up for these types of events. One thing that came as a bit of a surprise was that we weren't able to attract top level decision-makers until we started charging for attendance. I guess it was the "you get what you pay for" mentality. A fee of $60-$75 seemed to work the best.

Marketing was done mostly through direct mail and you had to send out a lot of invitations to get a good size group. A good response rate would be 5-10% and only about half of those would show up if we didn't charge a fee. Although it took a great deal of work, we were able to attract a level of decision-maker that had been very difficult for us to reach through other means. Additionally, the attendees had pre-qualified themselves as prospects by their interest in attending."

– Malcolm St. James, BioTech Industry

You can solicit attendance through telephone marketing calls or through direct mail. Allow 6 weeks prior to the event to begin your marketing campaign. Plan on contacting your list of prospects at least twice. To encourage action give them some incentive to sign up early. "To allow for maximum audience participation seats are limited." "First 50 people to register receive a free audiotape of the program." If you like, you can offer the tapes for sale in the back of the room to those who did not qualify for the promotion. This service is typically offered at all large association meetings and is a nice way to reinforce the value of the program.

The following letter is an example of a mailing I sent out to solicit registration for my Telephone Tactics for Business Professionals seminar. Although the letter references another program that I conduct, I've found that it's equally effective with both those who are familiar with my programs, as well as those who aren't.

Dear Colleague,

One of the most popular parts of my **Power Prospecting** program is the time we devote to the development and practice of *an effective telephone presentation*. During this segment participants use our prospecting structure to develop a telephone presentation that is specifically designed to grab the attention of the prospect and result in either an extended conversation, a subsequent meeting or a returned call (if the message is left on voice mail).

Lots of us are intimidated by telephoning someone "cold", but that doesn't have to be the case. If you've prepared what you're going to say, feel confident about the content of your message and are prepared to handle the likely objections, telephone prospecting becomes both a lot more comfortable and productive.

The only complaint that I ever get about my **Power Prospecting** program is that participants wish there was more time to devote to the telephone prospecting segment.

Thus, I'm holding a special 3-hour program on telephone prospecting skills on August 23rd from 9:00 am-12:00 noon at the Marriott Hotel in Atlanta. This session is specifically designed to focus and drill down on developing your individual telephone prospecting presentation. I'm not teaching a "canned" approach to telephone prospecting but rather giving you a structure so that the end result is compelling, intriguing and delivered "in your own voice". This program is designed to allow lots of opportunity to practice, receive feedback and develop replies to overcome likely objections in a highly professional manner that doesn't resort to any cheap sales gimmicks.

Naturally, in order to accomplish these objectives the class size is going to be extremely small to maximize the learning opportunity. The fee for the morning program is only $125 per person if you send two or more individuals, and includes all the seminar materials. If you're one of the first 10 to enroll you also receive a free follow- up phone consultation to further enhance your telephone prospecting skills. Those of you who have attended my programs in the past know first hand that my sessions are crammed full of information that you can actually use and apply the next business day. No fluff and lots of meat.

I thought that you or other members of your sales team might be interested in attending this program. If so, I'd encourage you to register quickly since a class of this type can't accommodate a large group of people, and I want it to be an extremely valuable learning experience for those who do attend.

If you want to register simply respond to this email or give me a call at 770-643-8566.

Hope to see you at the program.

Mark

PS: Don't forget that if you're one of the first 10 to enroll, you also receive a free follow-up phone consultation. This is an opportunity to further practice your telephone presentation, receive feedback and practice with me overcoming the common objections you're likely to hear. I'll even audio tape our session and send you the tape so you can reinforce the valuable learning from our time together.

Making Sure You Buy the Right Prospecting Contact List

T he success of both your phone solicitations and your mailings will depend upon the quality of the contact lists that you use. There is no shortage of list brokers, and the quality ranges from abysmal to very good. No contact list is going to be 100% accurate and some industries are more difficult for the list brokers to keep current than others are. For example, if you purchase a list of very small businesses, it will have a lower level of accuracy than if you're marketing to the Fortune 100. Small businesses simply change, are sold or go out of business at a rapid rate. Similarly, a list of high technology companies will be more difficult to keep accurate than a list of manufacturers, due to the volatility of the technology industry. As a general rule, a list that is about 80% accurate should be considered a good list.

Once you purchase a list, give it a quick review to see if there are any glaring errors. For example, I once purchased a list that had Louis Gerstner (at the time the Chairman and CEO of IBM) as the local sales manager in suburban Atlanta. One of the best list brokers I've used is InfoUSA. Visit them at www.infousa.com. Ask for Mark Ferguson and tell him I recommended you. He's done a great job for me over the years and I'm sure you'll be pleased with the service he provides you.

You can also use outbound telemarketing services to get the word out about your programs. I've tried numerous vendors over the years and was never happy with the results. They were either way to slick, canned, inept or salesy in their approach. Out of sheer frustration I decided that if I couldn't find the type of service I wanted, I'd start one of my own. If you're involved in business to business sales give me a call or email me at info@consultingexperts.com, and I'll be happy to discuss what we offer.

Successful Networking Strategies

L et's now spend some time on the subject of networking. With all that has been written about networking one would think that we are a nation of highly skilled networkers. Unfortunately, this is not the case.

"An important lesson in networking is that you have to keep at it. I made the mistake a few years back of thinking that I had built my network to the point where I thought I knew everyone who could be of help. What I forgot is that a network is a constantly changing group of people. People change jobs, move or die. If you don't keep building the network it will shrink and amazingly fast."

— *Douglas Cumberland, Shipping and Transportation Industry*

Unfortunately, many people approach networking from the perspective that the overarching goal is to meet as *many* people as possible. This follows the premise that everyone one meets might know someone who could be a customer. In theory that makes a certain amount of sense. The plumber might know an executive who might have a need for your services. While the scenario is not inconceivable, the larger question is where do you want to spend your time? With a group of plumbers or with people who are more likely to directly buy your products? It's a matter of playing the odds and where you want to invest your time. The key to successful networking is not only working the meeting in a productive manner, but also making sure that you're going to the right events. What constitutes the right events will vary enormously depending upon what you sell and who you sell to. Thus, success in networking is equal parts strategic (What meeting should I attend?) and tactical (What do I do once I'm there?).

Introducing Yourself: How to Prepare Your Log Line

In order to get the most out of the time you invest in networking you've got to be able to communicate what you do in a way that is short, concise and memorable. Sounds simple, but it's amazing how many people aren't able to do this. When people describe what they do it tends to be either way too technical for the average person to understand, or way too general.

A too technical description of what you do is especially harmful if you're trying to sell to the top-level decision-maker. Most top decision-makers are fairly far removed from the detailed technical aspects of their business. If they were once technologists, they have likely moved on and are now dealing with a myriad of issues including sales, production, finance and human resources. They have specialists on their staff who deal with the technical implementation issues. Thus, if you approach them with a highly technical description of what you do, it's very understandable for why they would immediately refer you to someone on their staff. Conversely, if you're too general, it's difficult to visualize what you do and as a consequence the level of interest will be minimal. Thus, you have to strike a balance between being too specific or too general.

For example, I recently met a fellow at a networking event. I asked him, what did he do? "I make people productive." What type of people? "Everyone" How do you do that? "Lots of different ways." As much as I might like to, I'm going to have difficulty being aware of situations that might call for his expertise. In a networking meeting you've got to be able to communicate what you do in a way that is short, concise and to the point. This is what's called your Log Line.

The term log line has its roots in the motion picture industry in which a two-hour movie is summarized into a single sentence. For example this is a log line: A South Carolina pacifist plantation owner joins the war for independence after a British officer murders his 15-year-old son. As you may have guessed, that's the log line for the movie, *The Patriot*.

Here's another: A fact-based sea yarn about a skipper of a Massachusetts swordfish boat that finds itself in the path of killer storms. That's the log line for the movie, *The Perfect Storm*.

What we need to do is to develop a log line that is specific enough, without being confusing to somebody who doesn't have our level of technical expertise. For example my log line is, "I specialize in working with sales teams helping them make prospecting for new business more productive and less frustration" This is readily understandable and encourages people to ask me appropriate follow up questions. How do I do that? What types of clients do I work with? My log line is the first step in ensuring that the person I'm speaking with has a clear understanding about what I do.

So, turn to a fresh page on your pad and let's prepare your log line. Remember that our goal is to create a log line that is simple enough so that someone who's not in your industry would easily understand what you do. Developing a log line for a fellow techno-speaker is not difficult. Preparing your log line so that someone, such as myself, can understand it, is more challenging. Now you may be thinking that this doesn't apply to you because, "I only talk with techno-speakers" That's only true if you're selling pretty far down the pipeline and don't have ambitions to sell at the more senior levels. To develop your log line write down answers to the follow two questions.

- I specialize in working with...(Who? Industry? Types of people?)

- I help these people to... (What? Satisfy what need? Achieve what goal? Avoid what consequence?)

Your log line is now 90% complete. All you need to do is combine the two sentences together. "I specialize in working with (Who?) helping them (To do what?)." You'll notice that my log line follows this format; "I specialize in working with sales teams, helping them make prospecting for new business more productive and less frustration." Remember that your goal is to strike a balance between being overly vague and mind-numbingly technical. A too general log line such as, "We bring good things to life" is as unhelpful to your networking efforts as a too jargon laden one, "We optimize channel distribution strategies to generate linkages and enterprise performance." (The person actually sold magazine advertising.) Remember that your goal is to be able to describe what you do in a way that is both understandable and elicits further interest. When you put together your log line, email it to me at mark@consultingexperts.com and I'll give you a free review and feedback.

How to Become a Brilliant Conversationalist By Asking Good Questions

S ome pundit once said that the key to being a brilliant conversationalist is the ability to ask good questions. Many people in my seminars say that one of the reasons they're uncomfortable at networking meetings is that they don't know what to talk about. My advice is to shift your focus. Don't worry about what to talk about, focus instead on asking good questions. You'll find that this is a helpful skill to develop for when you are in any social situation.

Questions I find particularly helpful to ask in networking situations include:

■ Who buys your services?

■ How would I know that a company has a need for your products?

■ Who are your major competitors?

■ How are you different from them?

■ What's your biggest headache?

■ How do you find new clients?

■ How can I help you?

I find these questions to be of benefit for a number of reasons. First, they're easy to remember and to ask. Secondly, they provide you with clues about how you might be of assistance to the person you're talking with. You never want to forget the concept of the favor bank. If I do you a favor it's expected that you will do me a favor. There are unfortunately people who don't grasp the concept of the favor bank. They're real good at receiving favors, but never repay them. Obviously these are individuals we will want to cull from our list of networking contacts.

I was doing a seminar recently for the military. The audience consisted mostly of master sergeants. We were discussing how things actually get accomplished in the army. One sergeant commented, "Yes, things get done to a certain extent because of the chain of command and rank, but from a practical standpoint, things get done by exchanging favors back and forth." The favor bank is not about being unethical or underhanded, but rather the sincere and positive process of trading favors. I have found that in order to be effective in organizational life you've got to embrace this concept.

The third benefit of asking good questions is that it leverages in your favor why most people attend networking events. In my seminars I'll ask attendees what does networking mean to them? Typically I'll hear answers such as: "To make new contacts." "To find new sources of business." "To meet people who may be aware of opportunities." In effect their answers all have to do with "me, me, me". Now there is nothing inherently wrong with those reasons, but it's important that we recognize this primary motivation if we're going to make the time we invest in networking productive. Since most people are at the meeting for "me, me, me" reasons, we need to let them tell us what they do *before* we attempt to explain what we do. If we immediately jump in and start talking about our work, it will fall on deaf ears since the person we're speaking with hasn't yet had a chance to talk about herself. Let's let her satisfy *her* objective for coming, before we attempt to educate her about what we do.

This is why asking good questions pays dividends. It's largely due to what the psychologists call the "mirroring effect". Put simply, the mirroring effect states that you will tend to ask me the same questions I've previously asked you. If you refer back to my suggested list of questions, you'll notice that they are not only good questions to ask, but also good questions for you to answer. The most effective way to get asked these questions, is for you to ask them first. The better the questions you ask the better the questions you'll subsequently be asked to answer. This is how to manipulate (and I use that term in the most positive sense) the initial networking conversation to our maximum advantage.

Remember that networking is an exercise in quality not quantity. Meeting a few people with whom you can build a productive relationship is much better than collecting a pocket full of business cards. Unfortunately, many people I observe at networking events seem to confuse quality with quantity. At the end of the day one may have an impressive collection of cards, but what exactly does one do with them? Certainly you want to meet as many people as possible, but you want to make sure that for every person you meet, you communicate how you can provide value. Think rifle, not shotgun.

Networking is time consuming. You must make a commitment to doing it on an ongoing basis if it's going to prove to be of any substantive value. It is not something that one does only when the pipeline begins to dry up. One of the more successful networkers I interviewed was Edmond Saris with the Software Company Axiom. He said, "Prospects must be nurtured by regular contact the same way you must water a garden regularly in order to make it grow." I think that is a very apt analogy, and one which I try to remember on a daily basis.

Different Networking Venues Worth Considering

A nother important part of the networking equation is to make sure that your networking activities are focused on the venues that are likely to be the most productive. You want to fish at ponds, which actually have fish. Prof. Tom Stanley makes the point that, "Ordinary sales professionals target ordinary prospects while extraordinary networkers target prospects who are opinion leaders of targeted groups."

Where do the decision-makers congregate? Wherever that is, that's where you want to be. As mentioned earlier, you'll certainly want to consider joining one or more professional associations. By professional associations I'm referring to the associations that represent the industry or market that you sell *to*, rather than the trade associations that represent the industry your company is in. For example, I do a lot of work with technology clients. Thus I try to become very involved in technology related associations. This is different than joining an association that represents my particular profession. I might attend a sales training conference to see what my competitors are doing, but quite frankly networking with my competition doesn't help me an enormous amount.

I got solicited from the American Society for Training and Development the other day. Very nice person on the other end of the phone. Her pitch was that if I paid thousands of dollars to attend the association meeting I would have the opportunity to "network with my peers". I didn't quite understand why that was a good thing to do. Sure there would be some training buyers present, but so would be most of my competition. That means that I would have to outspend them in my booth space if I was going to get any reasonable share of visibility. I'd rather go to events where there isn't quite so much competition.

For example, if I go to a manufacturing trade show, I'm often the only sales trainer there. Even if my competition shows up, they certainly aren't there in the mass numbers that they would be at events that cater to the training profession.

Another group that may be worthwhile investigating for its networking potential, are charities. One of my clients is a small sporting goods manufacturer trying to market to the NFL. My client became heavily involved in the United Way not only because he believed in the work that they do, but also because this is a charity that has strong ties with the NFL. In a relatively short period of time he was able to make contacts with several senior level decision-makers who would have been extremely difficult to meet through other means.

If your market is in a defined geographic area, civic groups may prove to be valuable. These include Rotary, Lions and Chambers of Commerce. One of my clients is a company that manufacturers a product used by accountants in many different industries. His sales strategy is to become very well known within a particular geographic market. Civic groups like these are a great way for him to build his business.

Still another venue to consider is continuing education programs. You can approach this from the perspective of teaching a class or enrolling in one where your fellow students might also be potential customers. Not only do you continue your own professional education but you can also pick up some valuable contacts as an additional benefit.

There are also formal networking groups. Passing leads and exchanging business cards are the primary purposes of these meetings. Many local newspapers publish listings of these meetings on a weekly basis. These groups tend to cater to small companies, so if your market is small businesses you may find these meetings highly productive.

Planting Your Networking Flag

T he key to becoming involved in any networking group is to pick one or two and try to get deeply involved. A common complaint that people have about joining associations is that they don't immediately have access to the inner circle. Although it would be nice if you were immediately asked to be a part of the leadership council, that's highly unlikely. All organizations have an inner circle and if all you do is simply show up to an occasional meeting, you can't reasonable expect to become a part of that group.

Once you've identified an association that you feel has potential, get involved on one of the committees. What committee is best from a business development perspective? Membership tends to be the most valuable committee since associations live and die on membership. You meet all the new people in addition to all the prospects that don't decide to join for one reason or another. Even if the prospect only shows up for one meeting you can add them to your contact list for your own personal follow-up activities. If you want to meet lots of people in the shortest time possible, membership is the way to go.

Here's another way to learn about groups that might be worth a visit. Many cities publish a weekly Business

Journal, which focuses on covering the local business scene. These business journals are now published in over 40 cities. You can find out if there is one in your city by visiting their web site www.bizjournals.com One of the particularly nice features of these journals is the weekly calendar of events that lists all the networking and association meetings taking place. Using this list, it's easy to identify groups to visit.

Another nice feature of the journals, and this is also true for the business section of your local daily paper, is the listing usually called "People on the Move". This section tells you about who has been promoted and who is in new assignments. It's a great way to keep track of the comings and goings of the people in your target market. When you see an interesting promotion or announcement don't forget to cut it out, get it laminated and send it off along with a note of congratulations.

Another great method to find potential associations is in your public library. The Directory of Associations lists national associations by both industry and function. You'll find that most of the associations have their head-quarters in Washington DC, but a quick call or email to the main headquarters will easily lead you to the local chapter in your town. You can also get on the web and go to Google and enter the name of the industry or function you're interested in. Finally, you can also try typing in www. (name of the association).org. I've found that this is a surprisingly productive way to immediately find the association I'm seeking.

Remember that the goal is not join as many associations as you possibly can. That's usually not a productive use of your time. It's akin to the networking strategy of trying to collect as many business cards as possible with no regard about who you're actually meeting. You must have reasonable expectations about associations as you must have about all of your prospecting strategies.

Once again turn to a fresh sheet of paper on your pad. What I would like for you to do is to list the groups that you currently belong to and write yourself some notes about how you might get more involved. If new associations come to mind that you might want to consider joining, this is a good time to jot those down.

Building Your Network. Who Do You Currently Know?

Networking requires an ongoing commitment to making new contacts and maintaining relationships with old ones. I think that most people are surprised at how many people they actually know but have lost contact with for one reason or another. You may find the following exercise to be helpful.

Who Do You Know?

- Whom have I received leads from in the past?

- Who sells to the same people I sell to?

- Who stands to benefit from the same events/circumstances that I do?

- Who do my competitors network with?

- Whom can I help?

- Whom have I helped I the past?

- Who wants to help me?

- Who do I know from previous jobs?

- Who do I know from school?
- Who else is a good networker?

Remember that if you do not keep expanding your networking base it will contract; and it will contract at a rate which is a lot faster than it expanded. One person I receive a lot of valuable leads from is Laura Schilling. She's a great networker and knows a lot of people. Although she's not directly involved in my line of work she is such a good networker that she's been a wonderful resource over the years. I'm sure you know someone like Laura Schilling. Now is an excellent time to make sure that valuable contacts, like the Laura Schillings in your life, haven't slipped off your radar screen.

Networking Tactics

Let's spend some time on the tactical issues involved in successful networking. I'm always interested in observing how people act at networking meetings. You can usually find at least one group of people who obviously knew each other before the meeting because they spend the entire time together. I suppose this is fine if one attends these events as an exercise in teambuilding, rather than an opportunity to expand one's client base, but they shouldn't complain that networking doesn't generate any new clients.

I also notice people who spend the entire time talking with people they've obviously met at previous meetings. Again, this is fine if the event is a social outlet for you, but it's unproductive behavior if you're really trying to build a network of new contacts.

It's natural to get intimidated if you arrive at a function and don't know anyone. However, the good news is that there are some specific actions you can take to make yourself feel more comfortable. Approach networking events with the assumption that most everyone there wants to make new contacts, even if at times it doesn't appear that way. Obviously, if you see two people engaged in a very intense conversation, intruding on that conversation is going to feel awkward. Your common sense will give you an accurate feel for when to introduce yourself and when not to.

I've found that at virtually all of these meetings, everyone is interested in meeting new people, they just don't know how to go about it. The easiest way to approach a group is to stand slightly off the shoulder of one of the group members and wait for an opening in the conversation. Use that lull to ask a question about what's being discussed. Don't insert yourself by initially introducing yourself. You will find that you will be received more favorably if you start off by asking a question. As with all networking activities this shows that you're interested in other people and that you're not a "me, me, me" type of networker.

Your goal should be to begin to build relationships. Nobody is going to buy your services right then and there unless you're selling something like pens out of your briefcase. You can always identify the networking rookies because they are trying too hard to push their services. Remember that the networking meeting is not a retail store where other people are there to buy. It's the first step in what will hopefully be a long-term relationship. Having said that, it is important to be aggressive about meeting new people and making sure that others are aware of what you do.

One of the traditions of all networking meetings is the exchange of business cards. This sounds fundamental, but remember that it's the little details that can make the difference. For example, you want to make sure that the business cards you give are stored in a different pocket than the business cards you receive. If you don't designate different pockets, you'll wind up handing the business card of someone you recently met to the person you're currently talking with. I find that simply putting the cards loose in my jacket or pant's pocket makes them a lot easier to distribute rather than fumbling with a business card case. Since I'm right handed, I put my cards in my right pocket and place other people's cards in my left.

Paying attention to even the smallest details can make the networking process easier and more productive. For example, take nametags. I've found that preparing your nametag in advance pays dividends. The nametags you get when you sign in for an event often aren't very good. They're either the fill-in-your-own-name variety, which isn't a good alternative for people like myself whose hand-writing is illegible, or they invariably tend to have the name of the organization in 48 point type and your name in 8 point type. These nametags give you a clear reminder of whose meeting you're at, but don't help you much in determining who you're talking to. I think the most frus-trating nametags are the peel and stick kind since they invariably become unraveled as time goes on. The solu-tion I've found works the best is to purchase clear name tag holders and insert either a piece of paper on which I've typed my name and company, or my business card.

The typical networking meeting consists of two parts, socializing and a meal. We've talked about socializing and the importance of not playing it safe by spending all your time with those you already know. Try to move around and not get stuck with people you don't want to get stuck with. A great way to get unstuck is to introduce the unde-sirable person to someone else. If your competitor is pres-ent, what better person to palm them off to? Other tactics include refreshing your drink, getting something to eat, or simply saying that you want to mingle and meet new people. While you don't want to be rude, you don't want to spend excessive time with people who aren't likely to be productive business contacts

The meal presents its own set of challenges. This part of the meeting can either be highly productive or a total waste of time. It depends upon who you're sitting next to. The challenge is that unlike the socializing part of the meeting, in which you can circulate from person to person, once you've chosen your seat, its difficult to pick up and move.

Over the years I've tried different strategies with varying degrees of success to increase my odds of sitting next to prospects with the most potential. For a while I tried to sit next to the person who was the most professionally dressed, but that oftentimes turned out to be someone looking for a job. Unfortunately, the unemployed aren't a good target for what I market.

The strategy that I've found works the best for me is to try to double my bet. It works this way. When I go to a net-working meeting I always carry a folder or portfolio. Sometime during the socializing part of the meeting I'll set the folder down at a seat in one of the front tables. This reserves my seat at a table where it's likely the dinner speaker or members of the board of the association are likely to be siting. When it comes time to sit down for dinner I'll go to different table which I also think has potential. If my tablemates meet my expectations, I'll retrieve my folder from the first table. If the group isn't what I hoped they would be, I can exit and go to my other chair which has been reserved by my folder. You only have a small window of time in which to pull this off. Obviously, you can't change seats after the meal has been going on for fifteen minutes. Generally, I've found that you've got about five minutes to check out your two seating options and make your decision.

Keeping Track of Who You Meet

All of our hard work during the meeting won't result in much if we don't keep track of whom we've met. This gets increasingly difficult once you start to attend networking events on a regular basis. One trick is to write some notes about the person you're talking with on the back of their business card. I generally do this in front of the person while I'm talking to them. I've found that people are flattered that I'm actually taking notes about what they're saying. The notes I take reflect common links such as, mutual clients, mutual hobbies or previous employers. I'll use that link when I follow up with the individual. Trying to find a reason to re-contact the person is crucial for developing the relationship. Relationships take time and a number of contacts to develop and a lack of follow up is the prime reason why networking activities so often don't pay long-term benefits.

I'll also give each person I meet a priority grade based on my first impression. Granted this is only a first impression, and it can often be wrong. However, if you're at an event where you're going to meet dozens of people, it's a helpful way to prioritize who should be followed up with first. I tend to call the top contacts and send emails or regular mail to the B and C contacts.

If you are going to follow up, it's important that you do it quickly. Within one week if at all humanly possible. New contacts have a very short shelf life, and it's amazing how quickly they'll forget having met you. Personally, I've found that there isn't much difference if you follow up via email vs. snail mail. Snail mail has the advantage of being highly personal, while email has the advantage of being quick. Email also has an advantage of increasing the likelihood of an immediate response. People who won't return my telephone call are often very responsive when I email them.

The question then becomes what do you say in your follow up letter or email? As with everything, there are good ways and bad ways to follow up. Here's a good way:

Dear _____ ,

Ever since the ACG meeting I've laughed every time I recalled your comments on small town Georgia. It reminded me of my own childhood growing up in a tiny community in Massachusetts.

Obviously in order to write this letter I wrote on the back of the person's business card "grew up in small town Georgia."

I also have a standard letter I'll send out if there wasn't a connection that came up in the conversation:

Dear _____ ,

It was a real pleasure to meet you at the XYZ lunch last week. I was quite impressed with the people I met. What was your impression? We didn't get a chance to discuss at length how I can be of assistance to you. Are there particular types of individuals or companies where I might be of some assistance in introducing you? Please let me know.

As you may recall, my firm focuses on working with sales professionals on making prospecting for new business more productive and less frustrating. I've taken the liberty to attach some information about our Power Prospecting program. Is there someone within your company aside from yourself that I should be contacting to introduce our services?

It was good to meet you. Please let me know how I can be of assistance.

Sincerely,

Conversely, you can have the budding relationship hit the proverbial brick wall by sending out a letter in which the emphasis is strictly on "me, me, me". For example, how many times have you received something like this?

Dear Mark,

It was good to meet you at the IAB meeting. If you ever need...

Here's one I received recently:

Dear Association Member,

It was a pleasure having the opportunity to meet you today and speak with each of you concerning your professional ambitions. I look forward to learning more about what each of you are involved in and hope to develop a stronger relationship with you in the coming months.

What's the problem with this letter? The "Dear Recipient" style of opening. Although it takes more effort to personalize a letter, it's definitely worth the time.

New Business Development. Are You Overlooking Opportunities?

Let's talk some about where your future sales are likely to come from. It's surprising how few sales professionals have really given much thought to this. Sometimes the answer is found through a simple brainstorming session to identify the common links that exist between your existing clients. Is there a particular industry they're in? A geographic location? Is there a particular person or job function that is the most interested in the solutions you provide? Sometimes this exercise leads to interesting conclusions. For example, one of my clients thought that their product was mostly used by the oil and gas industry. However, after completing a brain storming exercise they realized that marketing managers, regardless of the industry they were in, were the target market. This realization radically shifted their networking and sales efforts.

This is an opportune time to think about your business in a similar vein.

■ Who else could use your services?

■ What are the common links that exist between your current clients?

■ Do you want to target primarily in your own back yard or expand to a different region of the country?

Write down on your pad of paper the answers to these questions.

Telephone Tactics: Developing Your Phone Presentation

W hy do we hate to cold call? It's universally the least favorite weapon in the arsenal and I've known people who will do everything humanly possible to avoid picking up the phone and making a call. In part, it's because we instinctively think of telephone marketers as those obnoxious folks who call us during supper to hawk long distance services. Plus, calling someone completely cold makes us uncomfortable, if not outright fearful. The good news is that there are precise steps we can take to make the process more productive and less uncomfortable.

One very helpful tool for building confidence and effectiveness is to develop a telephone presentation. I avoid using the word "script" because that makes us think of something that is canned, salesy or not natural. A good telephone presentation should be both persuasive and natural. Taking the time to develop a presentation has the added benefit that you can refer to it any time you make a call. We've all had times when we've been "on" and the words effortlessly flow out of our mouth. Conversely, we've all experienced situations when we're "off" and can't string together two sentences to save our life. Having a prepared presentation ensures that we achieve a consistency in how we come across over the phone. It also serves as a safety net and helps reduce the anxiety we feel about picking up the phone and calling someone cold. So turn to a fresh sheet of paper and let's get started.

Your phone presentation is going to consist of five parts which we'll construct piece by piece. These parts are:

- Who you are/ Who you work for
- What you do
- Credibility from others
- Why you're calling
- Permission to ask questions

Part One: Who You Are and Who You're With:

This is pretty straightforward. The key here is that we want it to be short. If you have a title that's impressive, by all means use it. I've found that if I say that I am a partner with the sales training firm Solution Resources, the level of receptivity is a little bit higher than if I call and just use my name. Naturally, if you have a title that pigeon holes you as a lower level employee, you'll want to omit it. This is why practically everyone who works at a bank is a vice president. Use your good judgement and you'll do fine. If you have any questions give me a call. Write down your "Who you are and who you're with" part of the presentation on the top of your sheet of paper.

Part Two: What You Do:

Now, once we have established who we are and who we're with, we want to move to part two. You've actually already prepared this part when we worked on developing your log line. It's important to remember that at this point in the conversation the prospect isn't really interested in how big your company is, how long it has been in business or how many offices you have. Even if they might be potentially interested, they're not interested right now. Thus, you want to forgo your natural tendency to establish your credibility at this point in the presentation. We'll do that a little later. What you want to do immediately after you introduce yourself is tell the prospect what you do. This is your log line. To reiterate what we discussed before, you want to use the format of, "I specialize in working with…helping them to…" For example what I say at this point in the presentation is, "I specialize in working with sales teams helping them make new business prospecting more productive and less frustrating."

Remember that this is a short, concise and immediately understandable opening statement that explains the service you perform and who you perform that service for. On your sheet of paper, write down you log line.

Part Three: Credibility From Others:

The next step is to build your credibility in the ear of your prospect. When we talk about building our credibility, we're talking about it from the prospect's perspective. We want to ask ourselves what would make the prospect comfortable with us? It might be recognizable companies you've worked with in the past. It might be the number of people you've worked with over the years. Perhaps it's the number of years your company has been in business, the size of your company, or it's scope of operations. For example, my credibility statement is, "For over the past ten years, I've worked with sales teams from companies including U.P.S., AT&T, and CitiGroup." I'll focus on mentioning companies that are in the same industry as the prospect. Again, we want to build our credibility based on what is going to be most credible in the ear of the prospect. Take a moment now and write down what your credibility statement is.

Part Four: Why You Are Calling?

The next part of our prospecting telephone structure is the, "why you are calling". This is the hook. The subsequent success or failure of your call will largely hinge on what you say at this point in the conversation. Again, using a structure ensures that you have consistency when you reach this important part of the presentation. Here's a format that works well for many individuals and is recommended by sales trainer Art Sobczak (www.businessbyphone.com).

> **I know from talking with other** (peers of the person you're calling) **that many of them are concerned about** (a need you believe the prospect has). **Based upon what you're now** (doing, using, or experiencing) **in this area of** (concern) **I may be able to help you** (reduce) **your** (problem) **while at the same time** (achieve) **your** (desired outcome).

The trick to making this an effective and natural sounding presentation is what words you put inside the parenthesizes. For example instead of the word **"reduce"** you might insert: save, consolidate, minimize, decrease, cut down on, eliminate, get rid of, lessen, cut, lower, soften, shrink, slice, trim, combine, or modify.

Instead of the word **"problem"** you might use: cost, trouble, difficulty, obstacles, annoyances, inconveniences, time, expenses, hassles, burden, work, labor, efforts, paperwork, worries or anxieties.

Instead of the word **"achieve"** consider using: strengthen, intensify, boost, increase, expand, add, grow, maximize, enhance, create, build, ease or help.

Finally instead of the term **"desired outcome"** consider using: profits, sales, dollars, revenues, income, cash flow, savings, time, productivity, morale, motivation, output, attitude, image or market share.

You'll want to experiment with different words so that you accurately capture the needs of your prospect and what you feel you offer as a solution. Look at the wording of this structure as only a starting point. If there are other words that resonate better for you, by all means use them. Now, go back to your pad of paper and write out a persuasive reason for why you are calling.

Part Five: Permission To Ask Questions:

The next part of our telephone prospecting structure is the permission to ask questions. The objective of any cold call is to try to get it to be a two-sided conversation as quickly as possible. However, we don't want to resort to any cheap or obvious sales gimmicks like asking how they are, three seconds into the conversation. Hopefully, what you've accomplished by this point in the presentation is to intrigue your listener enough so that he or she is willing to spend a little more time on the phone with you. We're a long way from making a sale, but we should be developing enough traction to engage the prospect in a dialogue.

Our strategy is not to simply start asking questions but rather to gain permission to ask questions. An effective way of doing this is to say**: "If I caught you at a good time, I'd like to** (discuss) **your situation to see if this is something that** (you'd like more information on)". Again, there are different words and phrases we can substitute for what are in the parenthesizes.

Instead of "**discuss** " you might substitute: ask a few questions about, review, go through or analyze.

Instead of the phrase "**you'd like more information on**" you might substitute phrases such as: would be of value to you, might be worth considering, you would like to discuss, would be of interest, or would work for you".

Again, go back to the presentation you're developing and write down what works best for you when you want to ask for permission to ask questions.

There it is. You now have a telephone prospecting presentation ready to go! Naturally, you'll want to practice and refine it so that it sounds natural coming out of your mouth and not like something that's being read off a piece of paper.

Asking Good Questions

T he questions we ask should line up with the benefits that we offer. Asking questions about benefits is much more powerful than *telling* our prospect about the benefits. For example, one of the benefits I offer is overcoming the fear of cold calling. While there is nothing inherently incorrect about telling my prospect about this benefit, it's much more powerful if I ask a question. For example I might ask, "Is anyone on your sales team uncomfortable, afraid or reluctant to make cold calls?" Using questions to communicate benefits is especially powerful because when you answer my question, you're re-enforcing in your mind the need that you have for my service.

You'll want to prepare lots of benefit questions because sometimes your prospect is likely to say "No, that isn't a problem." If you have a number of them prepared, you can quickly shift gears and inquire about an area where there is an actual need. Another advantage of asking specific benefit questions is that even if you miss the mark it's quite likely that your prospect will respond with a *specific* need that they actually do have. For example it would be quite common to hear, "No, my sales team is very willing to pick up the phone and make the call. The problem they have is how to overcome objections." The more you ask questions that focus on a specific solution you offer, the more likely you are to hear specific needs.

I'm a firm believer that the key to effective sales, whether it's done over the telephone, or face-to-face, is the ability to ask good questions. I don't think successful sales people need to have a predominate personality type in order to be successful. I've met rainmakers who were backslapping extroverts and those that appeared extremely shy and introverted. What they all had in common is the ability to ask good questions. So, let's spend some more time on good ways to ask questions.

A good question starts with a good beginning. You'll want to use language that doesn't put the listener on the defensive but encourages them to enter into a dialogue. I've found the following to be effective ways to preface a question:

- Do you ever notice that you are…?

- When was the last time you needed to…?

- What do you do when…?

- How would you handle…?

- Is anyone in your group…?

- What happens when…?

- What problems does it cause you when…?

- How often…?

Now would be a good time for you to start developing some questions that are based on the benefits you offer. Turn to the page on your pad where you earlier listed the benefits that your product or service offers your clients. On a fresh sheet of paper I'd like for you to construct a question that would correspond to that benefit. Once you've completed this exercise, I'd encourage you to print out these questions and hang them next to the telephone presentation you developed. This will enable you to quickly refer to both important pieces of information when you're making your prospecting calls. I think you'll find that having both of these sheets available will make you a lot more comfortable and confident in making calls to people you've not spoken with previously.

Use Questions To Address Objections

You can also address many objections by asking questions. Remember it's virtually impossible for your prospect to admit that they are wrong. However if you can provide them with additional information that they have not previously considered, you may be successful in getting them to change their minds. Asking good questions is the key to accomplishing this. The more your prospect talks, the greater the likelihood that he will reveal what the real issues are and provide you with information that you can use. Remember that your approach should be to handle the call as a conversation in which you are discussing a *problem*, not an objection. Your focus should be on finding a *solution*, not purely overcoming the objection.

Start out when you hear an objection with phrases like:

- "Let's talk about that question."

- "Let's discuss that."

- "That's an interesting comment. Let me be sure I fully understand what you mean."

- "Tell me more about that."

- "That's a very logical concern for people in your business."

- "I can certainly understand why you would say that given what's going on in your industry."

- "That's a question we hear quite often from other executives in your industry."

- "That's a valid concern in light of the issues you're faced with right now."

Questions to Address Specific Objections

When they're buying from another supplier:

- "Under what circumstances would you consider using an alternative supplier?"

- "What type of contingency do you have for an emergency situations when your current supplier may not be available?"

- "What prompted the decision to go with them?"

- "What would you like to get that you don't have now?"

When they say they want to think about it or ask you to call back later:

- "I'll be happy to. What's going to make that a better time for you?"

- "Let me ask you a few questions now so I'm better prepared for the next time we speak."

- "I'm glad you liked it. Which aspects did you feel are the most beneficial to you?"

- "I agree, this does seem to fit with what you need. What do you think you're going to do?"

- "What will your decision be based on?"

- "What's the likelihood that this will be what you choose to do?"

- "What's the next step after you've done your analysis?"

- "What concerns do you still have?"

- "What's causing you to hesitate?"

- "What questions are still unanswered for you?"

- "What are you still unsure of?"

- "Is it because there's something that needs to happen

before you buy, or that you don't see enough value in acting right away?"

When price is the objection:

- "What amount did you have in mind?"

- "What are you comparing the investment to?"

- "Putting cost aside for the moment, what would you like to see accomplished?"

- "Are we talking about just the price itself, or the long term value of the solution?"

- "What are we being compared to?"

- "What price did you feel would be appropriate for what you're looking to receive?'

- "Take price out of the picture for the moment; do you like this solution better than others you've seen?"

- "Under what circumstances would you be able to justify the investment?"

- "Is price your main concern or are you looking at other factors too?"

When they ask you to send information:

- "I'll be happy to. So I can highlight the most relevant sections for you, can you give me an idea of what specifically you might be looking for?"

- "If you like what you see, what will happen?"

- "By when do you think you'll have had a chance to review the materials so we can speak again?"

- "When do you feel you'll be ready to make a purchase?

- "When should we speak again?

Ending the Call and Moving the Sale Forward

No telephone prospecting call is complete until you and your prospect reach agreement on the next step. This will vary from person to person. It might be a meeting, a follow-up phone call or sending information. Whatever you want to have happen, ask for it with confidence. Don't waffle. Don't hide what you want under a ton of fluff. I find a phrase such as, "Based on what we've discussed, I really think I can help you achieve (your particular need), and I'd like to suggest (a meeting... a follow-up phone call...that I send you some information)." It's very important that if your next step is to send information, that you establish a specific date for when you will follow up. Otherwise it's far too easy for the momentum of the sales process to slow down considerably.

Leaving a message on voice mail

So what happens when you get voice mail? The first question is whether you want to leave a message. Although there are different opinions on this, I don't think that there is any disadvantage to leaving a voice mail message. If it's well crafted and communicated in a professional manner, your message serves as a highly effective advertisement for the benefits you offer. Conversely, if I'm returning a person's call I try not to leave a voice mail message unless it's absolutely necessary or if I know that I will be difficult to reach. One tip on leaving a message is to provide them with specific information on the best time to reach you and any alternative numbers where you can be reached. I'll usually leave both my cell phone number and my email address in an attempt to minimize telephone tag.

What type of voice mail message to leave? I'd recommend that your voice mail message be very similar to the one that you would communicate to a live individual. Start off with who you are and who you work for. This is followed by parts two, three and four of the structure; What You Do, Credibility From Others and Why You Are Calling. Up to this point you haven't deviated from the presentation you've already prepared. When you get to part five of the presentation, Permission To Ask Questions, you'll want to modify your presentation slightly. I substitute the phrase, **"I'd like to set up a time to** (discuss) **your situation to see if this is something that** (might be worth considering). Again, you'll want to experiment with the words you put in the parenthesize to determine what sounds best for you.

I then leave my contact information and the best time to reach me. Since only 10% of calls to new prospects get returned (if you're lucky) you'll need to be persistent. My strategy is to call every ten days. If after the tenth try I haven't heard back I'll call once a month. I vary my message every third time I call. Sooner or later you will be able to break through, although it can be frustrating at times. That's the reason why it is so important to make lots of prospecting calls. There is a lot of truth to the old saying that rainmaking is a contact sport — the more contacts you make, the greater the likelihood of success. My largest client required over 15 calls before I finally spoke to a live person. It was certainly worth the effort. As long as your message is professional in tone and substance you don't have to worry about being perceived as a pest.

Using Creative Excuses To Stay In Touch

O nce you've established the initial contact the focus now shifts to staying in touch. This requires a bit of creativity. The challenge is that you can't simply say, "Want to buy my stuff?" or words to that effect every time you call. That obviously gets quickly redundant for both you and the person you're calling. However, what exactly *is* your reason for calling? Think about your reasons or excuses for calling as falling into one of two broad categories; industry intelligence (or gossip if you want to be completely accurate) and helpful favors. The latter draws upon the prospect's perspective or knowledge and are designed to make them feel important.

Industry insights/gossip obviously requires that you are knee-deep in a particular industry. Otherwise, the chances of your being privy to information that isn't in the general domain is pretty slim. If you become known as someone who, "knows what's going on in our industry", you'll find that you get a lot of your calls taken and returned. This is another reason for specialization, since from a practical standpoint it's extremely difficult to develop insider insight across multiple industries.

The second excuse is to directly appeal to the ego of the person you're calling. This works off the premise that most executives like to be made to feel that their opinions and insights are important. This strategy is particularly effective if you get in the habit of giving speeches and writing articles. For example, in the process of writing this book I've been on the phone on a regular basis with numerous prospective and existing clients. Calling them serves a couple of purposes. One is that I get great insights and ideas for the content of this book. The second is that it gives me a reason to introduce myself or stay in touch. Granted a number of the calls don't produce new insights. However, that's not the point. The real benefit is that I have a legitimate reason to contact prospects about a subject that is directly linked to my business. That's invaluable.

The same process can be applied when you prepare to give a speech. Not only do I call prospects for ideas, quotes and suggestions for the speech-I also invite them to attend. I would estimate that over the past 10 years less than 1% of the people I invite actually show up. But, that's not the point. Inviting them to my speech is another excuse to stay in touch. Additionally, by inviting them to attend a speech, I must be viewed as a knowledgeable expert by the group that invited me. This does nothing but raise my credibility in the eyes of those I invite, regardless of whether they actually attend or not.

Other excuses I've used recently to stay in touch include: thanking a prospect for a referral, sending congratulations on a promotion, requesting the name of a vendor, referring a possible job candidate, asking for help on a professional association project, providing information on a potential customer, asking for an anecdote for use in speech, sending an article clipped from the paper and offering a lead on a job search.

In Conclusion: Using All the Weapons In Your Arsenal

Rainmakers, top guns, business builders, new-logo builders, call them what you will. If we're a sales manager, we want to hire them. If we're a sales professional, we want to be one. In the end, what makes a rainmaker different from the rank and file business developer?

Certainly, hard work is unsurprisingly a part of the equation, but it isn't by any means the most significant factor. I believe what makes a successful rainmaker was pretty well summed up by General Dwight D. Eisenhower when he was asked why the allies were successful at D-Day. Eisenhower first said that the most difficult part of the whole operation was the willingness to *commit* to the invasion. He went on to say that the ultimate success was a result of a coordinated effort using all of the resources available; artillery, paratroops, the navy, ground troops, the airforce and even spies. This is what it takes to be a rainmaker. The willingness to make a *commitment* to prospecting combined with strategically using *all* of the resources available. I firmly believe that this is why some succeed, while others fail at new business development.

From a practical perspective we don't know precisely which tactic will generate a specific piece of new business. It could be a speech, an article, a telephone call, a referral, whatever. Since we don't know what will precisely tip the business to us, the successful power prospector plays the odds by doing some of everything. Luck is a factor, but similar to playing any casino game, we should do everything we can to put the odds in our favor. Granted, we will tend to gravitate to some prospecting strategies more than others based on our personality and what we're most comfortable doing. That's natural. However, top rainmakers don't exclusively rely on the methods they are innately comfortable with. While the term "outside the comfort zone" is overused, in this case it really does apply. We need to learn how to parachute from the plane, pilot the jet, storm the beach and fire the artillery.

You now know the strategies and tactics that top rainmak-ers use to build their businesses. The next step is to go out and use them. Good luck!

Mark Satterfield

About the Author

M ark Satterfield is the founder and president of Solution Resources. Since 1992 he has consulted with companies in a wide variety of industries on how to make prospecting for new business less frustrating and more productive.

Prior to founding his firm, Mark held executive positions with PepsiCo and Kraft Foods in addition to having served as the director of career services for the Graduate School of Business at Emory University.

In addition to his consulting work, Mark has written over 250 articles on personal and career development which have appeared in publications including the *Atlanta Constitution,* the *Los Angeles Times* and numerous professional, trade and technical journals. He is also the author of five books including, *"How to Negotiate the Raise you Deserve"* and *"Business and Career Etiquette".* The book *Power Prospecting* is also available in a comprehensive audiocassette package.

Mark has an undergraduate degree in English from Washington University and a master's degree from Norwich University. He is a two-time winner of the Dow Jones award for writing excellence, the AMA award for training excellence and has been included in *Who's Who Finance and Industry, Who's Who in Higher Education, Who's Who in the South, What Color Is Your Parachute* and many other biographical guides.

Mark can be reached at (770) 643-8566 or mark@consultingexperts.com.